RODA

a Downland village

S.B. Publications

Published by S. B. Publications
c/o 19 Grove Road
Seaford
East Sussex BN25 1TP

ISBN 1 85770 183 6

View of Mount Caburn from Virginia Woolf's garden studio

Text, design, typesetting by JEM Editorial
6 Castle Banks, Lewes BN7 1UZ
01273 471485/JEMedit@aol.com

Printed by Tansleys The Printers
19 Broad Street, Seaford
East Sussex BN25 1LS
01323 891019

Glorious tints and textures

As if ordered by an artist, Rodmell meanders picturesquely from the slopes of the Downs to the water meadows of the Ouse, its single street fringed by a pleasing jumble of houses and cottages built in every variation of vernacular architecture.

In January 1859 the Earl of Abergavenny gave land and £50 towards the cost of building a church school. The total cost was £150.
The school opened in April that year with forty-five children on the books. Parents paid 2d a week each for the first two children, 1d thereafter.

Picture postcard pretty, Rodmell is almost certainly unique among Sussex villages in that it has no gift and craft shops (actually no shops at all), no tea gardens, no village green and, to all appearances, no church – for twelfth century St Peter's is tucked away behind trees at the end of a tiny twitten.

Yet it is these apparent deficiencies that make Rodmell the haven of peace and beauty that draws writers, artists and musicians to live here, and brings discerning visitors back time and again to experience the rural idyll.

A century ago the villagers were mostly farm workers, with a few domestic servants, blacksmiths, millers, wheelwrights and shop

The Old Rectory

workers. They tended to have large families, and often there were eight or nine children in a tiny cottage that today would be considered barely adequate for a couple. The population now is much as it was at the end of the nineteenth century – but the same number of people, only a handful of whom have work related to the land, occupy twice as many homes.

Some observers are saddened by the change, within just a few years, from self-sufficient farming community, cowpats and all, to sanitised middle-class dormitory – but, without the commuters, the civil servants, the lawyers and media workers who are the new villagers, Rodmell's lovely old buildings could have fall-

Deep Thatch Cottage

en into decay, been torn down and replaced by the Sixties semis that have

Rampantly lush cottage gardens

destroyed other Sussex villages.

Here there are thatched and timbered little cottages straight from a fairy story; weatherboarded and tile-hung homes converted from ancient agricultural buildings; houses of weathered brick; others rendered and prettily painted; quaint flint row homes and new houses lovingly built from traditional materials to blend

seamlessly with the old.

Squared, knapped flint faces the imposing former rectory and, capping a sturdy old building on a bend is a deep, wavy (oddly le Corbusier) thatched roof.

The rich palette of materials and colours – the ochre, sage and burnt sienna tints of lichen on the old clay tile roofs; time-weathered oak beams faded to a soft grey; the sharper, counterpointing greys of flint and slate – is complemented by banks of snowdrops on a bleak January day, drifts of daffodils in spring and glorious, rampantly lush cottage garden flowers all summer long.

The lych gate

There are glimpses of paddocks and fields over old flint walls, of horses contentedly ambling through the buttercups, of mellow farm buildings; there is the scent of woodsmoke and, breaking the great stillness and quiet of the village, are the cluckings of domestic fowl and the twittering of a myriad birds – even on a cold winter's day.

One of Rodmell's

Flints

attractions is Monks House, the former home of Virginia and Leonard Woolf. It is administered by The National Trust, but is open for only two afternoons a week during the summer. Unusually, for a National Trust property, it has no gift shop or café, and only a small (terribly unobtrusive) car park. On Saturdays in summer, when Monks House is open, tea and biscuits are served in the Village Hall by volunteers from the village hall committee.

Rodmell is a linear village, straddling the little C7 Lewes to Newhaven road, just over three miles south of the county town.

To the west of the road the village street, now called Mill Lane, climbs steeply to the summit of the Downs. Mill House, tucked behind the forge, was the last property up the lane until 1928.

Between the wars agricultural depression forced the sale of farm land, and homes started

Rose Cottage

crawling up the slopes of the Downs. Virginia Woolf, who used to walk on the hill when the lane was a mere farm track, thought it 'iniquitous' that the Downs could be spoiled in this way.

Yet the well-designed new houses instead added to the pleasing village tapestry, and even the former local authority homes, set in a crescent around a little green, present a charming picture.

On the cricket pavilion behind the church there is a copy of the famous Calling Time weather-vane at Lords Cricket Ground. The Rodmell version was made by the village blacksmith, Frank Dean.

Origins of a village

Until the early years of the twentieth century, the Sussex Downs were a magical green world of gently undulating hills, bisected by deep dry valleys and carpeted in short, springy turf fragrant with the mingled scents of cowslip and sweet violet, aromatic wild thyme and marjoram, heady meadowsweet, scabious and rampion.

Few today know the range as anything but a patchwork of cereal fields, brown-ribbed in winter, soft green in spring and every shade of gold in summer – each a beautiful sight, but at the cost of both the aesthetic balance of the Downland landscape and the ecology of traditional chalk grassland.

But these days there is a move back to sheep husbandry, a practice that, over centuries, created the Downland once so beloved of writers and artists, and now, on the hill above Rodmell, woolly flocks close crop the turf, encouraging regrowth of traditional wild flowers and herbs.

A tracery of early field systems on Mill Hill, and a cluster of barrows, are the only reminders of Rodmell's earliest inhabitants. The village established on the lower slope of the hill was Saxon, and the name Rodmell

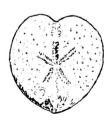

Fossils of the chalk Downland

7

almost certainly comes from the early English for red mould, although some say it could mean the mill on the road.

In 1066, when the conquering Normans laid claim to the village, it was called Redmelle or Ramelle. A century later it was Redmeld, after which it was variously known as Rudmill, Radmyle, Radmeal and Rodmill. By the middle of the seventeenth century it was Radmell or Rodmell.

Until the Conquest, Rodmell was in the Hundred of Homestreu, but after the Battle of Hastings Sussex was divided into rapes, north to south, each with a fortified castle and an escape route by sea to Normandy.

Rodmell and other villages on the west bank of the Ouse were in the Rape of Lewes; those on the east bank, in the Rape of Pevensey.

The annual tax was paid in herrings

The Domesday Survey of 1086 shows that Ramelle, owned by the Norman lord William de Warenne, Baron of Lewes, was the size of thirty-three hides, and was valued at £37. The village had a population of 130, a church, eleven saltpans and forty-four haws in Lewes, valued at twenty-two shillings and rated for 4,000 herrings.

Remains of the Priory of St Pancras, showing workmen cutting through the ruins to build the rail line from Brighton

The role of the river

Near Rodmell, a barge plies between Lewes and Newhaven c1890

The River Ouse rises at Slaugham millpond, in Sussex, west of the M23, and travels thirty miles south and east through lush pastures and woodland, past pretty villages, picturesque old houses and cottages, to the sea at Newhaven 250ft below.

Until the early years of the twentieth century the river was busy with commercial traffic. Sloops and brigs were built at Lewes; agricultural produce from the valley farms was carried by barge upstream to Lewes market, downstream to Tidemills or to cargo vessels in Newhaven; clay from the pond at Piddinghoe went to Asham Cement Works; bricks made at Piddinghoe were taken up-river to build the massive Ouse Valley railway viaduct near Balcombe; from the Twenties, tons of cement were shipped from the Asham wharf to destinations around the country.

The herrings were an annual tax, and the haws were houses or other property, owned by Rodmell's burgesses, who lived in Lewes, and who paid the herring tax.

A major influence on Rodmell from the eleventh century was the Priory of St Pancras, built by William de Warenne and his wife Gundrada below the Lewes hilltop on which they had their castle. It was the mother house of the Cluniac order in England, and occupied a vast area of land. The church alone was said to be larger than Chichester Cathedral.

Work began in 1087, with Caen stone shipped from Normandy. The de Warennes' priory became famous across Europe and attracted many pilgrims and royal visitors.

A shepherd of the Downs with his flock and dogs

Because it was bounded on the north by Lewes and on the south by the water meadows, St Pancras, unusually, had no farm land of its own, and the valley farms prospered by supplying produce to the monastic community. It may be that the monks set up a farm of their own at Rodmell, on the site now occupied by Northease Manor School. Where the footings of one of the converted farm buildings are exposed slightly above ground level, a string of large stone blocks, possibly Caen stone, is visible.

In 1537 Henry VIII ordered the dissolution of the monasteries, and today only remnants of walls remain where the great priory once stood.

The de Radmeldes, who probably named themselves after the village, held the land by military service from 1150 to 1499, when the male line died out. They lived in the manor house, Hall Place (demolished in 1838 as it was falling apart).

Legend says that the manor was afterwards granted by Henry VIII to his wife, Ann Boleyn, whom he had beheaded in 1536, and that her daughter, the future Virgin Queen, visited the village often. The improbable story relates that the path the princess walked from the manor house to the Lewes road was ever after called Princess Walk. The path still exists and now it is called Prince's Gap.

The village remained a holding of the barony of Lewes through the

centuries, eventually coming into the ownership of the Abergavenny family in the seventeenth century.

The lord owned the village and all the houses and farms in it. Every manor had a reeve, the lord's officer, who collected the rents and accounted to the owner at the end of the year.

From the Middle Ages the village economy centred on sheep and corn, with each farm being linked to a sheep down (common or enclosed) with an arable acreage on the valley flank above the floodplain, and an area of water meadow.

The sheep flock was maintained as a 'moving dunghill', being folded at night on the part of the arable land left fallow, so that ultimately the success of the corn crop depended on the sheep.

A typical farm or holding was in strip form from the river to the summit of the Downs, so that each included areas of greensand, brookland, clay and chalk.

John Ellman of nearby Glynde improved the Southdown breed of sheep, producing an animal world-famous for its wool, its succulent meat, hardiness and low feed costs. The sheep were driven to market in Lewes, and to the great sheep fairs at Findon.

From the eighteenth century Rodmell farms were taking in cattle, driven from the west of England, to be fattened on the rich water meadows and then sold in London.

'Rodmell . . . has been greatly affected by the change in Agriculture. Formerly its population was one third as large as at present. There were 6 farms in the village occupied by freeholders, besides other freeholders – a thriving community. Now, the farms have gradually been sold and merged into one. We have neither resident owner or occupier. Mr Brown holds Northease and lives at Landport Lewes. Mr Stacey rents Rodmell Farm and lives at Kingston. The absence of the Masters has a very deteriorating effect on the men. The walls in the village are crumbling and broken – the cottages are in a sad state. There is hardly one good sound comfortable cottage in the village.'

From the diary of the Robert Rosseter, Rector of Rodmell, 1891

The advent of steam-refrigerated ships, bringing cheap meat and dairy produce from New Zealand (whose great sheep flocks, ironically, had been founded on Ellman's Southdowns) and Australia, and grain from the United States, exacerbated the agricultural depression of the

Music of the sheep bells lost from the Downs

last quarter of the nineteenth century. The competition from abroad also included vacuum packed and canned foods, and corned beef from South America.

Traditional farming methods began to disintegrate and many labourers, whose jobs had also been hit by improved mechanisation, left the land for life in the towns.

Flocks were reduced drastically and the music of sheep bells was lost from the Downs. For hundreds of years sheep had contributed to the specialness of the South Downs, and with the sheep went the flowers, the birds and the butterflies.

Farmers equipped themselves with machinery that made intensive cultivation of the hill tops a practical proposition and, within two or three decades, Ouse valley farms had turned principally to fattening bullocks and to dairying.

Commuters and weekenders bought the farmhouses and cottages, and the whole socio-economic structure of the valley changed.

The population figures remained much the same – but those who lived in the villages, and in particular in Rodmell, were different people.

Smuggling days

Used to see the tubs brought on horseback 3 or 4 on a horse. Half a pint of gin for 6d. Landed at Saltdean and Chingap – a lot of tubs used to lay in a barn in the Rector's garden. Some say they used to be hid in the valley between the Chancel and the Chapel roof of the Ch.

From the diary of the Reverend Pierre de Putron, Rector of Rodmell, 1858

Rodmell's windmill

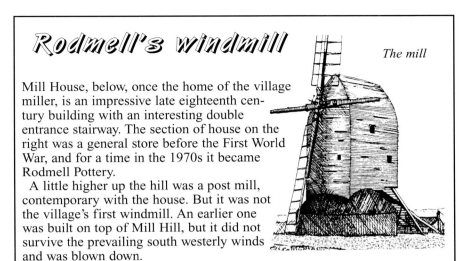

The mill

Mill House, below, once the home of the village miller, is an impressive late eighteenth century building with an interesting double entrance stairway. The section of house on the right was a general store before the First World War, and for a time in the 1970s it became Rodmell Pottery.

A little higher up the hill was a post mill, contemporary with the house. But it was not the village's first windmill. An earlier one was built on top of Mill Hill, but it did not survive the prevailing south westerly winds and was blown down.

Use of the replacement mill for grinding flour declined towards the end of the nineteenth century, and by 1912 it was working with only two sweeps, and was considered worthless. Skinner, the last miller, sold it for scrap, the timbers fetching 2/6d a cubic foot. Frank Dean has childhood memories of playing with friends among the millstones left lying in the saucer-shaped hole where the mill had been, and the thrill of turning the stones over to find snakes' eggs.

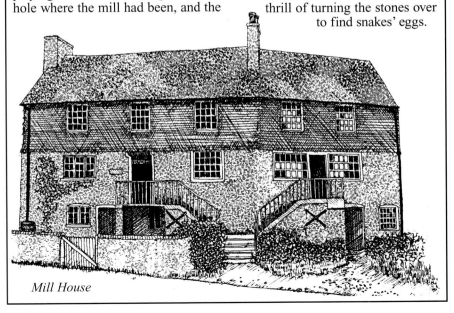

Mill House

Rodmell's gift to St Richard

From the churchyard there is a splendid view of Mount Caburn, which has a Romano-British hill fort on its summit.

The Norman church of St Peter was built in the twelfth century on the site of its Saxon predecessor, which had been part of the possessions of King Harold, and had passed, with the manor, to the de Warennes.

The second William de Warenne gave the church to the Priory of St Pancras in 1095. The monks, in their turn, presented it in 1252 to St Richard de Wych, when he was Bishop of Chichester. There was some legal problem about terms of the gift, and the matter went to arbitration. But the ownership was confirmed and the Bishop of Chichester is still, today, the patron of the living.

Every hundred years or so since then there have been additions and alterations. The church was heavily restored, some say over-restored, by the Victorians.

It retains its twelfth century font with its oak panelled cover from the time of Henry VIII but the ironbound chest for vestments, left to it by Richard Weyvyle in 1417, has disappeared.

14

The miller and the church bell

Many years ago, it is said, the village miller, driven to distraction by the sound of a church bell made by the local blacksmith, cursed bell and blacksmith. He consulted a witch, and was told that the only way to stop the hideous cacophony was to tie hair from the Devil's tail to the bell's clapper. Defeated, the miller gave up but, years later, lost in a thick sea fog over the water meadows, he was saved from possible drowning in the Ouse by the sound of the church bell guiding him home. Thereafter the miller never again complained about the church bell, and in his gratitude he presented St Peter's with a new chime of bells.

Norman window in the chancel

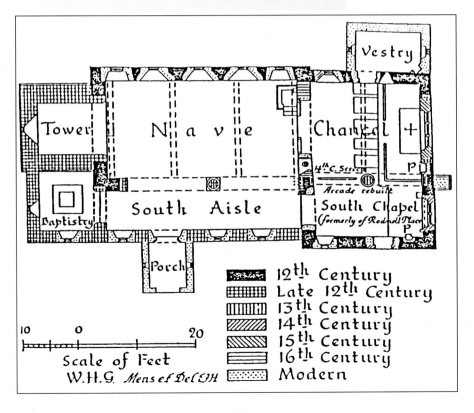

Tower

Nave

Chancel

Vestry

Baptistry

South Aisle

4ᵗʰ C. Screen

Arcade rebuilt

South Chapel (formerly of Rodnel Place)

Porch

- 12ᵗʰ Century
- Late 12ᵗʰ Century
- 13ᵗʰ Century
- 14ᵗʰ Century
- 15ᵗʰ Century
- 16ᵗʰ Century
- Modern

10   0   20

Scale of Feet
W.H.G. Mens et Del 9H

Bloomsbury in a Sussex village

Virginia Woolf

Molly MacCarthy coined the term Bloomsberries in 1910, and the name Bloomsbury Group came into existence a year or so later.

Vita Sackville West, Virginia Woolf's one-time lover, called it the Gloomsbury Group.

On Monday, September 1, 1919, two horse-drawn farm waggons trundled across the level crossing and the little bridge over the Ouse at Southease, carrying the contents of Virginia and Leonard Woolf's weekend place, Asham House, to their new home in Rodmell.

Virginia, and her sister, the painter Vanessa Bell, had taken a lease on Asham, on the slope of Itford Hill, in 1911, and established there an outpost of Bloomsbury.

The Bloomsbury Group was a coterie of post-Victorian intellectuals, writers and artists who first met in the London home of the young Stephens – Virginia, Vanessa and their brothers Thoby and Adrian. The quartet, orphaned in young adulthood, had set up home in Gordon Square, Bloomsbury, and thus the name of a London borough became shorthand for an attitude to life and art.

A few weeks after taking the lease on Asham, Virginia married the writer Leonard Woolf, and they spent part of their honeymoon there. Vanessa gave up her share of Asham in 1916 when she found Charleston Farmhouse at nearby Firle, and moved in with her husband Clive, sons Julian and Quentin, the painter Duncan Grant and his lover David Garnett. Grant and Garnett were conscientious objectors (to the 1914-18 war), and were found work on a local farm.

The lease on Asham came to an end after the

war. The Woolfs were anxious to keep a retreat in the Lewes area, Virginia especially, as her sister was now well established at Charleston.

The butt end of an old windmill

On impulse, while in Lewes one day, Virginia saw, fell in love with and bought The Round House. 'It's the butt end of an old windmill, so that all the rooms are either completely round or semi-circular,' she wrote to Dora Carrington.

The Round House is in Pipe Passage, a tiny twitten that follows the line of the old town wall. It is the base of a corn mill built in 1800 that was little used and was converted into a house in 1819.

Leonard was not with her when she paid estate agent Wycherley £300 for the odd little cottage. Indeed, it was some time before he was able to get away from London to inspect his new home, and when the couple did look it over it immediately became obvious that Virginia had made a mistake.

But all was not lost, for on the way back to the railway station to return to London, they saw a poster advertising the auction of Monks House in Rodmell 'an old-fashioned Residence and three-quarters of an acre of Garden (with possession)'.

The Woolfs knew the house, for often they had crossed the river and railway line at Southease and walked over the water meadows, up past Monks House, to buy cigarettes and tobacco in Rodmell's village shop. Peering over the boundary wall in the church twitten, Leonard had envied the owner the lush garden, the orchard, the

Sale particulars for Monks House, and Rodmell forge.

Monks House

Virginia wrote in her diary, on first inspecting Monks House: *'The rooms are small: the kitchen is distinctly bad . . . There's no oil stove and no grate. Nor is there hot water, nor a bath and as for the E.C. (earth closet) I was never shown it.'*

But she added: *'These prudent observations were forced to yield to a profound pleasure at the size and shape and fertility and wildness of the garden.'*

outhouses and stable.

On their instructions, Mr Wycherley put The Round House back on the market, and agreed to bid on their behalf at the sale in The White Hart Hotel. They set a limit of £800, and were nervously present as the price quickly reached £600. They were then in competition with only one other bidder, but eventually the house was knocked down to the Woolfs for £700.

Monks House is a plain house, a long, low, unassuming building, weatherboarded and with a singularly ugly extension, beneath a steep slate-tiled roof.

Monks House, first recorded in 1707, when it was held by Jane de la Chambre, was without piped water, electricity, gas or a sewage system when the Woolfs moved across from Asham. It was overrun by mice, primitive in the extreme,

The dubious extension

18

cold, damp and draughty.

For most of the 18th century the house had belonged to the Cleere family. They sold it in 1796 to John Glazebrook, who owned the mill higher up the village. In 1877 the house was bought by Jacob Verrall, Surveyor of Highways, Assessor and Collector of Taxes, Overseer of the Poor. It appears that until this time the house had been named after the families who owned it. Jacob Verrall called it Monks House, possibly through a tenuous connection with the Priory of St Pancras in Lewes. The last prior, Robert Peterson, held the living of Rodmell from 1553 until his death two years later.

Some partitioning between the nine small rooms was removed to create six larger rooms,

'What more comfort can we acquire? ... I enjoy my luxuries at every turn and think them wholly good for what I am pleased to call my soul.'

Virginia Woolf, in her diary, when mains electricity was installed in 1931

and over the years the Woolfs improved the house, installing a hot water system, a bathroom (paid for by the success of Virginia's book *Mrs Dalloway*, and doing away with the earth closet) and electricity. In 1929 profits from *Orlando* enabled them to have the dubious extension added. This consisted of a second sitting room on the first floor and a bedroom for Virginia on the ground floor – accessible only from the garden.

The house was never luxurious, even after the Woolfs' Hogarth Press achieved success. The carefully preserved interior – pots of geraniums in the windows, as Leonard always had, matches and tobacco on a table, a book by a chair – illustrates the simple life the Woolfs lived in

Richard Kennedy's drawing of Virginia Woolf with the habitual roll-up she had between her lips. She smoked a tobacco called My Mixture.

Sussex. The walls are still the particular shade of sea green Virginia insisted upon, and the odd, haphazard mixture of furniture and furnishings, which includes fine antique pieces, items designed and decorated by Vanessa Bell and Duncan Grant, and oddments picked up secondhand, show that the writers were little concerned with comfort.

It is, perhaps, a tidier house today than it was during the fifty years of Woolf occupancy. Julian Bell, Virginia's great nephew, remembered 'a maze of waist-high piles to be negotiated every time you crossed the room – books interspersed with manuscripts, magazines, ashtrays, sometimes pets'.

Jim Bartholomew, son of the Woolfs' gardener, Percy, remembered the same untidy piles of books and papers. The pervading smell, he said, was of cigarette smoke, woodsmoke, old bindings and apples.

Angelica, Vanessa's daughter by Duncan Grant, described the atmosphere at Monks House as 'concentrated, quiet and mysterious', and Nigel Nicolson saw it as 'rambling, untidy, hugger-mugger'.

In the first few years Virginia was unhappy at Monks House, but over time she grew to love her home and the village. In her diary in 1940 she wrote: *'When I think of M.H. when we took it – when I think of the E.C. in the garden & the cane chair over a bucket, & the dogs barking; & how I hated the village – which has become familiar & even friendly. Arent I on the Committee of the WI dont I go to meetings on a Monday?'*.

The dogs she mentioned were the fox terriers that Kathleen Emery bred next door at Charnes Cottage. Virginia also detested the church bells

Leonard Woolf in the garden of Monks House.

on Sunday – those 'cursed Xtian bells' she called them. 'The Xtian religion,' she wrote, was 'silly and repulsive'.

Leonard, on the other hand, was extremely happy, especially with his garden. He was an enthusiastic and knowledgeable horticulturalist, and had three very large glasshouses ('Leonard's crystal palaces', Virginia called them) against the school wall. A wooden shed in the garden was Virginia's writing lodge.

'They were both hard workers, professionals,' said Jim Bartholomew. 'I had a great deal of time for Leonard. He was a shy, helpful man. He did things quietly and sensibly.'

When, in later life, Jim became chairman of the parish council, Leonard offered his services as clerk (he served for seventeen years), and his home for council meetings. 'It was warmer than the village hall, and we didn't have to pay for it,' Jim said.

Frank Dean recalled Leonard as 'a smashing bloke'. 'He had a pretty violent temper, but he was a generous, nice man.

'He would moan like blazes if the village children got into his garden to steal his apples, but he would then take a big trug full of apples into the school for the children.'

In 1930 Frank's father installed a petrol pump in front of the forge, and Frank, then fourteen, was usually at the pump on Saturdays when the Woolfs drove up in their secondhand Singer for their weekly six gallons. The cost was 9/6d. Frank checked the tyre pressure after filling up, 'and then Leonard always gave me a ten shilling note, and waited for the sixpence change. Then he gave me half a crown for doing the tyres! It was typical

Drawing by Richard Kennedy of a Bloomsbury country walk with Virginia Woolf in the foreground, Mount Caburn in the background.

of Leonard. He was very generous.'

Virginia, Frank said, was very attractive. 'She

Wrinkled stockings full of taters

used to wear these bohemian clothes and big, floppy hats, and she had wrinkled stockings with holes – showing the taters, my sister used to say.'

Virginia delighted in long, solitary walks over the Downs and through the water meadows, where she was observed one day by actor/author Dirk Bogarde, who was on a boyhood fishing expedition from his home near Alfriston. 'She was tall and thin, with a long wool-ly, and fairish hair which

The writing lodge

looked rather wispy,' he wrote in *A Postillion Struck by Lightning.* Perce, one of the village characters with him, said: 'Bloomin' nuisance her. Always up and down the river she is, like a bloomin' witch . . they do say she's a bit do-lally-tap.'

With the Woolfs in residence in Rodmell, the village became a magnet for the writers, thinkers and artists of the Bloomsbury Group. Vanessa Bell, Duncan Grant and John Maynard Keynes (who had bought Tilton, near Charleston Farmhouse), were often over from Firle, and London friends came for relaxing weekends in the country, to stroll on the Downs and play croquet and bowls on the Monks House lawn.

When the Second World War began in September 1939 Leonard and Virginia made Monks House their full time home for the duration. Their London home was bombed and they sent Carvills, the Lewes removal firm, to salvage what remained of their books and furnishings and bring them to

Sussex. They rented space in the Bottens' farmhouse for the furniture, and took a room for their books in Mill House.

Virginia had suffered a number of breakdowns in her adult life and the threat of invasion worsened her frail mental health. She and Leonard learned that they were numbers 115 and 116 on a Nazi hit list of prominent people who were to be killed when the Germans arrived. In May, 1940, they considered gassing themselves in the garage, but decided against it.

Leonard joined other villagers on fire watching and air raid precation duties, and Virginia joined the Women's Institute. She wrote that her contribution to the war was the sacrifice of pleasure, by which she meant that she suffered agonies of tedium at WI meetings and was bored by the village women whose minds were 'so cheap, compared with ours'.

Virginia was fascinated by village gossip, yet did not understand people who were 'not one's own kind', and she could be cruel and thoughtless. She marvelled at the 'bloodless servitude of the domestic poor', and she sacked her servant Nellie Boxall when she became old and ill.

Leonard was kinder, although he, too, had no qualms about sacking employees for less than adequate reasons, as he did his gardener of more than thirty years, Percy Bartholomew. In his autobiography, Leonard wrote that Percy left his employ when he became blind. The family told a different story.

'Professional gardeners have a code,' Percy's son Jim explained. 'They will supply the kitchen with vegetables, but won't allow the kitchen to help itself. The cook did. She went out and picked the peas. Dad went in and told her off, she complained to Leonard and Dad was summoned.

'"Percy, you'll have to

Cast lead bust of Virginia Woolf by Stephen Tomlin in the garden of Monks House

Cast lead bust of Leonard Woolf by Charlotte Hewes in the garden of Monks House

go," said Leonard, and Dad went.' Evidently, good cooks were harder to find than good gardeners, and those who had one were always anxious never to offend the cook.

Percy lost more than his job when Leonard sacked him; he also lost his home. Some years earlier the Woolfs had bought Park Cottages. Housekeeper Louie Everest lived in the left cottage and the Bartholomew family in the right cottage.

While Virginia had been co-opted, albeit unwillingly, into the WI, Leonard was happy to mix with his neighbours and take a fuller part in village life. As well as being parish clerk, he was a school manager and founder member of the horticultural society. He held Labour Party meetings in Monks House and lectured for the WEA.

On March 28, 1941, Virginia wrapped up warmly in her fur coat, took her walking stick and set off across the brooks. Those who saw

her that morning took little notice as they were accustomed to seeing the eccentric Mrs Woolf walking alone over the fields and Downs.

The scene then was not as peaceful and quiet as it is today. At Asham, on the opposite bank of the river, was a noisy cement works 'the size of the Albert Hall', belching out a white dust that coated the hedgerows and trees. Beyond, Virginia would have seen the crater of a chalk quarry scarring the hill above her beloved Asham House.

At the river bank Virginia filled her pockets with heavy stones and walked into the water. Her body was not found for another three weeks.

Frank Dean, who was among the village men called out to search for Virginia when she did not return home, believes her body may have become trapped in one of the deep holes where the fences go down into the water. They prevent cattle walking around from one field to another at low tide.

An exceptionally full tide on April 18 may have dislodged the body which floated upstream towards Glynde Reach, where it was discovered by a party of young cyclists.

'I have a feeling I shall go mad in these terrible times,' Virginia had written in a note left for Leonard. 'I hear voices and I cannot concentrate on my work. I have fought against it, but cannot fight any longer.'

The funeral arrangements were handled by Frank Dean's father. Virginia was cremated in Brighton and her ashes buried beneath one of the great elms in the Monks House garden.

Leonard lived another eighteen years. The artist Treckie Parsons, who lived at Iford, became Leonard's companion in his old age, and she used Virginia's writing lodge as a studio. In his will, Leonard left her Monks House, but she did not want to live there, and sold it to the University of Sussex, which later passed the property on to The National Trust.

A stroke felled Leonard in 1969, and he died at home on August 14. His ashes were buried beneath a second elm. Virginia's elm fell, some years later, in a gale, and Leonard's elm succumbed to Dutch elm disease.

The house and garden are administered and largely maintained by a tenant for The National Trust. Monks House is open to the public from Easter until the end of October, on Wednesday and Saturday, 2-5.30pm.

The River Ouse opposite Asham

25

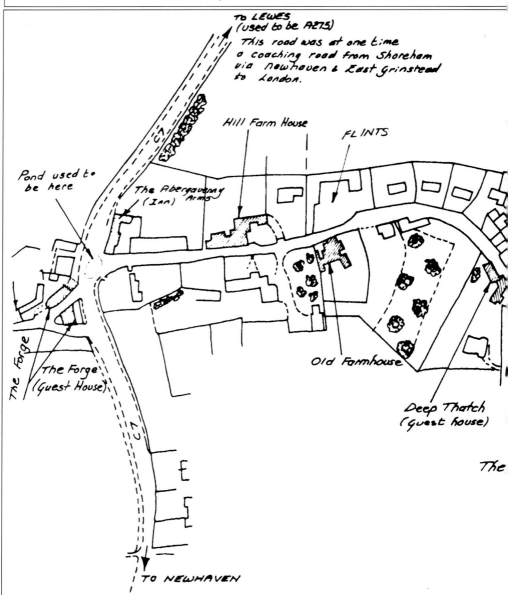

TO LEWES
(used to be A275)

This road was at one time
a coaching road from Shoreham
via Newhaven & East Grinstead
to London.

Hill Farm House

FLINTS

C7

Pond used to
be here

The Abergavenny
(Inn) Arms

The Forge

The Forge
(Guest House)

C7

Old Farmhouse

Deep Thatch
(Guest House)

The

TO NEWHAVEN

26

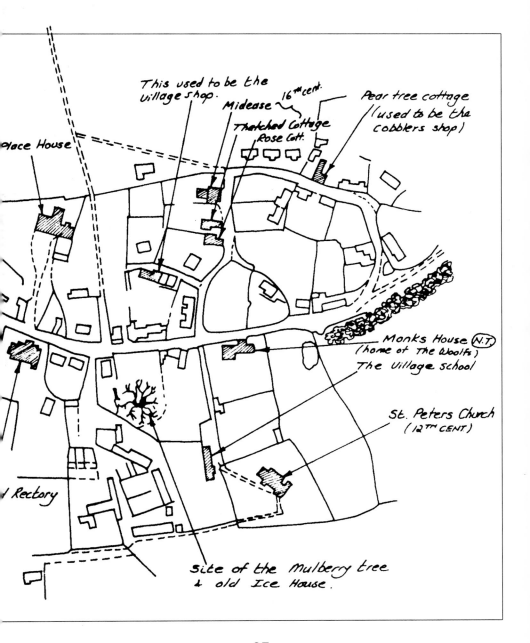

This used to be the village shop.

Midease — 16th cent.

Thatched Cottage
Rose Cott.

Pear tree cottage
(used to be the cobblers shop)

Place House

Monks House (N.T.)
(home of The Woolfs)
The Village School

St. Peters Church
(12TH CENT)

Rectory

Site of the Mulberry tree
& old Ice House.

John Morton

Now We Are Sick

Hush, hush, Nobody cares! Christopher Robin Has Fallen Down Stairs

J B Morton

Of pints and poems

Between the world wars there were two rival literary cliques in tiny Rodmell – the Woolfs and their Bloomsbury Group, and the beer-drinking, cricket-playing journalists, poets and novelists who gathered around Edward Shanks, James Murray Allison and John Morton.

These included John Squire, a gifted poet, and editor of the *London Mercury,* the poets Siegfried Sasoon and Edmund Blunden, Clennell Wilkinson, Hilaire and Peter Belloc.

Murray Allison, a wealthy Australian, an author and a backer of magazines, farmed for some years at South Farm. He lived with his family at Hill Farm House, which he had converted from two cot-tages, and he used the barn over the road (now Barn House) as a garage, electric light plant and potting shed. Allison later converted and moved to Old Farm House, nearby, where he kept open house for aspiring poets and writ-ers.

Edward Shanks, the assistant editor of the *London Mercury,* was the then owner of Charnes Cottage, next door to Monks House. When in London he shared a flat with John Morton – Beachcomber in the *Daily Express* – and was responsible for introduc-ing Morton to the village.

Morton, who bought his own cottage in 1922, made his name with a novel, *The Barber of Putney*, about his experi-ences in the trenches in

28

the First World War. He went into journalism and took over the *Express's* Beachcomber column from its founder D B Wyndham Lewis.

Gentle satire and surreal humour flowed from his pen for the next fifty years. He delighted in poking fun at pseuds and was deeply unpopular with many a literary set.

Allison arranged an annual cricket match between the villagers, and the Invalids, a team of visiting literary people from London. (The first Invalids team was made up of those injured in the First World War, and today the club still plays an annual match with the Rodmell side.)

Almost always the Invalids were beaten by the Rodmell eleven. Sabotage was suspected as Allison laid on lunches featuring mountainous beef puddings and endless barrels of beer.

'The village side can always stand his lunches better than we can,' the Invalids grumbled.

On the day of the match the pub did a roaring trade, and afterwards there was a big gathering at Allison's house.

Ballade of the Rodmell Cricket Match

Our new rolled pitch is gleaming in the sun
Without those blemishes that caused dismay;
Save where the boys have hacked it up for fun
Or where the moles have gambolled at their play.
On with the game; what though in disarray
We stagger back – four wickets down for three?
Last year's tail lives to wag another day –
Bring me the village bat and you will see.

Swift as a bullet from a sporting gun
Lithe as a panther leaping on its prey,
Cecil has grabbed another stolen run,
And Jack is bowling at both ends, they say.
No ball! Ten up! Six wickets down. O.K.
Once more it looks as if it's up to me
Sardonic Percy says I look distrait –
Give me the village bat and you shall see.

The score piles up – somebody's slammed a one
And run it out: Rodmell is going gay.
Hugh with a zest that's rather overdone
Has stumped the umpire, and his loud hooray
Recalls the slumbering Major to the fray.
And now begins a kind of jamboree
Of overthrows. You think we're still at bay
Give me the village bat and you shall see.

J B Morton

Rodmell Village

Rodmell has continued to attract arts and media people through the decades, and among today's residents are musicians, writers and artists – including Celia Berridge, illustrator of the popular Postman Pat children's books.

When he became a resident of Rodmell, Morton judiciously joined the village side.

Virginia Woolf objected strenuously to these people playing cricket on the pitch behind her home.

'Somehow,' she said, 'that the Downs should be seen by cultivated eyes spoils them for me'.

There was no social contact between the Allison-Morton group and the Bloomsberries. Clenell Wilkinson, it is reported, once boomed a jovial 'Good morning' to Virginia Woolf across the village street, and she was so startled that she fainted. And Eleanor Jebb, Belloc's daughter, revealed that the beer-drinking cricketers, to annoy the Woolfs, often left empty beer bottles on their doorstep

The group split up in the late 1920s when the Allisons moved away to Hampshire, selling Old Farm House to a military man, Guy Westmacott. Allison died in 1929.

Peter Belloc, Hilaire Belloc's second son, married in 1927 and left the group. He was killed on active service in 1941. Morton, too, was married in 1927.

Northease Manor School

Imposing Northease Manor, the largest property in Rodmell, is believed to have Norman origins. The first recorded settlement on the site on the northern boundary of the parish was a farm, almost certainly belonging to the Priory of St Pancras at Lewes. Nothing of such early occupation today remains above ground.

The complex of buildings, occupied by an independent co-educational school for pupils with dyslexia, includes the essentially Queen Anne manor house, set on an older cellar built of massive chalk blocks, a flinty Tudor barn in which ancient ships' timbers support a deep thatched roof, and a magnificent range of 18th century, flint-built agricultural buildings.

During the Second World War Northease Manor was used as a convalescent home for wounded Canadian servicemen.

In the early 1960s it was

The central Queen Anne manor house

31

bought by David Carter to become a home and school for children with learning difficulties.

Carter, an aeronautical engineer, recognised the problems caused by dyslexia many years before education authorities made any special provision for children who were affected, and he aimed to catch the children with above average potential but below average performance, who were then falling through the education net.

He created a unique independent school that wanted to do something special – and achieved a special school that happens to be independent.

When the school opened there were six pupils. Now there are ninety, around sixty-five of whom are boarders.

Carter died unexpectedly within a few years and his new headmaster, Roger Dennien, appointed in 1971, put together a group of interested parents, staff and well-wishers who bought the school from Carter's widow Joanna – in the teeth of fierce competition from the Roman Catholic Church, which wanted the manor for a seminary.

A trust was established, and then a charitable foundation to continue Carter's mould-breaking work.

A vineyard in the valley

Behind Northease Manor School the White Way leads for a mile or so over the Downs to Breaky Bottom, where Peter Hall planted a vineyard in 1974.

This is not one of those tourist trap vineyards with a craft centre in the bothy, a café in the byre, madrigals in the barn, morris dancers on the lawn and a shop selling the product by the bottle. There are no diversions for visitors to Breaky Bottom, other than a wonderfully panoramic view of rolling hills from the top of the Downs, and they turn up not for the bottle, but for the case.

The White Way, it must be said, is a rather inadequate farm track, deeply

'My aim is to make the best possible wine and hang the commercial consequences.'

Peter Hall

Breaky Bottom

Dry White Table Wine

Estate grown and bottled by Peter Hall
Breaky Bottom Vineyard, Rodmell, Sussex, UK

Produce of United Kingdom

75cl   11% vol

Breaky Bottom labels, above, were designed by eminent wood engraver Reynolds Stone.

rutted in places, potholed and extremely muddy in wet weather.

As a young man Peter, an agricultural graduate, took a job at Northease Farm where the farmer, Harris Robinson, asked him one day to go over the hilltop to Breaky Bottom to tend some sheep, and there, in a hidden, silent, Downland valley, he found a tiny shepherd's cottage, and an old flint barn, both derelict and abandoned.

At the time Peter was living in a rented room in Brighton and rising at 4am to get to work. He fell in love with Breaky Bottom and asked the farmer if he could take it on. Harris Robinson agreed, negotiating a rent of six shillings a week.

The cramped little cottage was virtually uninhabitable, with no services except water, which came from a standpipe outside.

Initially Peter bred pigs on his thirty acres in Breaky Bottom, but in the early 1970s he was inspired by reports of English grape-growing pioneers, and he planted the valley with Muller Thurgau and a few Seyval Blanc.

Soon he favoured Seyval, and replanted, creating the distinctive Breaky Bottom French-style dry white wine.

'Seyval Blank is well suited to the style of wine I try to make,' he says. 'It is very clean, not too Germanically fruity, more vinous in character and with a fairly aggressive acidity when young. The wines need two years at least to mature, and are really on song after three or four years.'

Against competition from wine-makers the world over, the 1990 Seyval won a Gold Medal in the 1993 International Wine Challenge and the 1992 won a Silver Medal in 1997.

Peter is now producing prize-winning Methode Champenoise sparkling wines. He says: 'The purists may tremble, but I have always felt that the hybrid Seyval Blanc would be eminently suitable for fizz, particularly growing on chalk, on the same geological outcrop which occurs in the Champagne region.'

Peter welcomes visitors, but it is best to call first, on 01273 476427.

East meets West at Breaky Bottom, where the line of the Prime Meridian passes through the valley.

Born in a barn

There may not be madrigals in the barn at Breaky Bottom but, a quarter of a century or so ago, the barn saw the birth of an opera company that has gone on to huge national success. Peter Hall, Trix Unsworth, Rebecca Meitlis and other committed friends put together a company that came to be known as New Sussex Opera, and the first performance, of *The Beggar's Opera*, took place in the barn with the audience sitting on straw bales and enjoying a glass or two of Breaky Bottom wine.

'It was magic,' says Peter, who is as serious about music as he is about making wine. Nigel Kennedy was one of many musicians who gave fund-raising concerts in the barn for the fledgeling company.

New Sussex Opera's production of *Peter Grimes* was, Peter says, 'our pinnacle, our triumph', and it attracted huge acclaim.

In the years since its birth in a barn, the company has gone on to independent fame and fortune.

The barn where opera was born

The village inn

Canadians manning the searchlight on Mill Hill during the Second World War took the Greenacres donkey to the pub one day, and gave it a bucket of beer to drink. Apparently, the legless ass, which had to be carried home, afterwards became the soldiers' regular drinking companion.

An inn or ale house existed on the site of the present Abergavenny Arms as far back as 1450, when it was the meeting place for local supporters of Jack Cade (with 20,000 men, Cade, an Irishman, had marched on London in that year to demand a fairer deal for farm labourers).

From the first half of the seventeenth century the pub was called The Old Bell, a name possibly given it when the church acquired its second bell in 1625. The name remained until the early nineteenth century when it was changed to The Abergavenny Arms in honour of the lord of the manor.

For a short period from 1976 the pub was The Holly, called after the then publican's daughter, but when it changed hands again, the locals persuaded the new owners to reinstate the old name.

In fact the inn started life as a barn, built in the traditional Sussex way of chalk blocks faced on each side with flints to keep out the weather. Many years ago the outside was

rendered, but the flint facing may still be seen on the inside.

The owners of the pub today are Mike Harman, a former Newhaven mayor, and his partner Ruth Stonell. They took over in 1997 and have returned the Abergavenny to the traditional village inn it always was before it became, for a short period, a must-be-seen-in fashionable restaurant.

In the upper eating area, which used to be an outside cattle shed, the original cattle troughs and hay mangers remain – and this part of the pub is said to be haunted by a young man who hanged himself when he was jilted by a village maiden. Ruth believes she has seen the shade of the sad lover, and some customers say they feel a presence.

There have been many extensions over the years. The yard that contained the well was covered over and became part of the inn, but the well remains – long dry since the water table dropped some eighty years ago and all the wells in the upper part of Rodmell dried up.

The view towards Itford Hill seen from Leonard Woolf's vegetable garden behind Monks House. The plot is still cultivated by green-fingered village gardeners.

Around the village

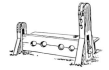

Briar Cottage

Despite its exceptional picturesqueness – around every bend an idyllic chocolate box scene – there is nothing pretentious or twee about Rodmell, where a spade is still a spade and not a horticultural implement.

There are few fancy names here, mainly straightforward labels to distinguish one property from another in a street without numbers.

Old Farm House and Hill Farm House were the homes and working places of long gone farming families. Barn House was a barn, converted to a house, Flints, a complex of flint-built agricultural buildings. Deep Thatch is a weatherboarded cottage with a splendidly deep thatch.

Navigation Cottages were occupied by employees of the Lower Ouse Navigation and Terrace Cottages, where The Loop joins The Street, form, as would be expected, a terrace – although earlier the homes were called Stocks Cottages because here was the site of the village stocks.

Around The Loop are some splendid

old timber framed and thatched cottages, and newer homes built to match the village style.

Park Cottages, also in The Loop, were bought by the Woolfs in 1929 for their servants. Annie Thompsett, the cook general, lived in the cottage on the left (and was succeeded by Louie Everest from 1934 to 1969) and Percy Bartholomew, the gardener, lived in the cottage on the right.

At the bottom of the village is Briar Cottage, formerly Court Farm House – the farmhouse belonging to the old manor house

The four poor cottages were built in 1810 to comply with a requirement that parishes provide accommodation for their poor, and a link with the past remains through a cottage called The Old Poor House. Granny Grey – Old Mrs Grey from Virginia Woolf's *The Death of the Moth* – lived in the lower cottage.

Across the church twitten from Monks House is Charnes Cottage, and beneath the branches of a massive, 300-year-old mulberry tree in the gar-

Thatched Cottage

den (seen over the white gate, or from the twitten) is an ice house built of brick and chalk blocks. This held carcasses for Hall Place, which stood on the site until demolished in 1836. The name Charnes comes from the de la Chambre family who occupied Hall Place from the seventeenth century. The mulberry is said to be the inspiration for Virginia Woolf's creation of Mulberry's, the florist's shop in *Mrs Dalloway*.

George Skinner, the last miller of Rodmell, gave two small cottages, which came to be known as Club Cottages, for use as a men's club. In 1920 they reverted to domestic use when a military hut, used at Seaford during the First World War as an officers' mess, became a new Club Room. Leonard Woolf was instrumental in setting up the hut, and Vanessa Bell, his Bloomsbury sister-in-law, came over from Firle to decorate the roof trusses. The Club Room was itself replaced when Rodmell Village Hall was opened in March 1960 by Leonard Woolf.

'I must write to Ottoline & ask her for the name of the little man who protects downs. This place is being risked & saved; & so perhaps will be again. Cutting down trees & spoiling downs are my two great iniquities.'

Virginia Woolf, on housing development in Mill Lane

Midease

The Old Rectory is a Queen Anne farmhouse much altered and modernised by Guernsey-born Pierre de Putron, the rector from 1858 to 1891, and the man responsible for the heavy-handed restoration of St Peter's Church – although without his intervention the church may well have decayed.

Only in Mill Lane, in the upper part of the village, are the fancier names to be found.

Until 1928 the Lutyens-designed Mill Furlong, Mill House, the flats, Forge House and the smithy were the only buildings above the main road. The flats were in a converted corn store built in 1850 when it was thought that the railway would be passing along the line of the Lewes to Newhaven road. In the event the line was built down by the river and the building was never used for its intended purpose.

James Allison bought it and converted it to flats for his farm workers, while the vacated farm cottages at South Farm became weekend places for his London friends.

Rodmell memories

Frank Dean

Blacksmith and farrier Christopher Dean came to Rodmell in 1910. He rented the smithy and Forge House for £26.10s.0d a year from the widow of Jacob Verall, who was living in Monks House.

After Mrs Verrall's death the smithy, the house, Monks House and other property in the village were auctioned, and Leonard and Virginia Woolf famously bought Monks House, while the blacksmith paid £540 for the forge, the house, stable buildings and an orchard.

Dean's son Frank was born in 1916. 'There were the Top Streeters (us and the children from the flats) and the Bottom Streeters,' Frank says of his childhood. 'I remember a village shop that sold most things, and a post office. Two bakers used to come out from Lewes with horse and cart, and one from Newhaven several times a week. Then when the motor vans came in there were weekly deliveries from a butcher and a fishmonger.'

In the years between the wars Ouse valley farms kept the forge busy with the repair and maintenance of agricultural machinery and tools; making shepherds' crooks, iron cart wheels, dipping, marking and tailing irons; and shoeing the great farm horses.

Christopher Dean and Son, as did many

41

The last Rodmell funeral when a farm waggon was used was in March 1940, for farmer Jasper Botten of Place Farm. Here Christopher Dean leads the procession. Prince, the farmer's horse, is led by Albert Thompsett, and the bearers are Jasper Botten's grandsons, the Carr boys.

rural carpenters, builders and blacksmiths, often diversified into the funeral business. 'We did funerals for Rodmell, Southease, Telscombe, Iford and Piddinghoe,' Frank recalls.

In 1930 the Deans set up a petrol pump on the main road to cater for the growing numbers of motorists. Eventually there were three pumps and a little kiosk.

The petrol station closed in 1995, but the pumps remain, a tangible reminder of the carefree inter-war years of the open road and the open tourer, and petrol at elevenpence halfpenny a gallon. The pumps and kiosk should, perhaps, be listed, and restored as an attraction of historic interest.

'Change in the village was so gradual it crept up unnoticed,' Frank says. 'When World War Two was over there were no horses about on the farms any more. All the farmers were modernising. Farms became larger, highly mechanised and had their own engineers and welding plants. Work died off for us, but then horses came back for recreation and we were kept busy shoeing.'

Frank retains strong memories of the Woolfs, and in particular he remembers March 28, 1941. 'The police came up for me the day Virginia dropped into the river. They needed ropes and grabs so I went down with them. The water was running very high and fast and we couldn't find her, although Leonard had found her stick floating in the water.

'I can see Leonard now, pacing up and down the river bank; he was a very brave man.'

Frank says that it was not until after Leonard died in 1979 that visitors began their pilgrimages to Rodmell to see the home of Virginia Woolf.

'It used to be mostly Americans, then Japanese. Now, I am surprised at how many Germans come to see Monks House,' he says.

Semi-retired, Frank has handed over the running of the forge to his son Roger, who has now been joined by *his* son, Stephen.

Adrian Orchard

In 1965 Adrian Orchard inherited his grandmother's cottage, Longthatch, and moved to Rodmell — but he has known the village well since his boyhood visits to his grandparents, and to his great aunt, Kathleen Emery, who lived at Charnes Cottage.

In the mid-sixties, he remembers, there were few cars and the village was still recognisably a rural community.

'There was a wonderful shop, run by Cissie Bennett, where you could buy everything. It was rumoured that after the health inspector called and declared the shop unhygienic, Mrs Bennett scrubbed everything with carbolic, and ever afterwards all the food, including the cheese and chocolate, tasted of carbolic.'

Adrian was secretary of the village horticultural society when Leonard Woolf was president. Leonard and Adrian's grandmother had started the society at the outbreak

The last village shop, set up in an outhouse of the 16th century farmhouse called Bybles, in a twitten off The Loop, closed in 1975.

43

of the Second World War, and the first meeting was held in Longthatch.

'Leonard was a marvellous man,' he says. 'I never realised at the time how important he was. He was very interested in the village and what was going on and he attended all the meetings. He was a very nice, unassuming man, very approachable, and he had tremendously wide interests. I remember how thrilled he was when England won the World Cup in 1966.'

Adrian, a retired notary public, now runs a small specialist nursery in nearby Southease. He has been interested in horticulture since he was a child, and he remembers Leonard's 'untidy, chaotic but wonderful' garden at Monks House, and his huge enthusiasm for gardening and for winning prizes at the flower shows.

The Orchards lived in Charnes Cottage after Miss Emery died, and were custodians of the underground domed ice house and the ancient mulberry tree.

The sixties heralded the end of Rodmell as a country village.

'It began when Denny Botten, the farmer, sold up,' Adrian says. 'Infilling with new houses began, farm buildings were converted and a different type of people moved in.'

Dorothy Medhurst

When another war started in September, 1939, Brighton-born Dorothy Maskell, an eighteen-year-old who knew only town life, went from dancing on the Palace Pier to mucking out in pungent farmyards.

Dorothy opted to join the Land Army because, she says, she liked 'the nice little uniform'.

She worked on farms around Lewes as part of Hobden's threshing gang – tough labour for a young town-bred girl. 'It was hard work, but good fun, and we all liked the life,' she says.

Dorothy was working for Guy Janson at South Farm, Rodmell, when Ron Medhurst returned from fighting in Burma, and was demobbed. Ron was a hersdman at Northease Farm. They married in 1947 and have brought up their five children in Rodmell.

'There were three farms in Rodmell when I came to live here. The house called Flints was farm buildings for Place Farm, and I remember Denny Botten, the farmer, letting his cows out of the yard in the mornings and they wandered down to his fields in the brooks by themselves. Someone used to go and turn them around when it was milking time.

'There were hardly any cars in those days, and the village children used to be out in the street, skipping and playing ball quite safely.

'Most of the cottages were owned by the farms, and quite a few of them were in a terrible state. Some were condemned after the war, and others were cramped, cold, damp and really unfit to live in.'

A few of the older villagers regret the change from the farming community of their childhood to the commuters' village that Rodmell is today, but Dorothy acknowledges that without the incomers, and their incomes, many of the buildings would have been lost.

The old ways could not have survived, she says. 'In my day the farmers worked with horses and carts; now huge tankers and trailers are used and the village street isn't suitable.'

Dorothy Maskell in the Land Army at South Farm, Rodmell, 1944.

Below, left, her husband Ron, who won many awards and cups at sheep fairs around Sussex. Now retired, Ron tends his immaculate allotment behind Monks House where Leonard Woolf had his vegetable garden.

Pauline Cherry

Pauline Cherry, the village's Parish Pump correspondent for the *Sussex Express*, moved to Rodmell in 1970.

'I remember going to a parish council meeting in, I think it was 1980, when they were discussing the possibility of a car park for visitors to Monks House,'

Pauline says. 'The councillors didn't really think it was needed. I told them that Virginia Woolf's fame would spread like fire across a stubble field, and they would need more parking – and I was right. They had no idea how famous Virginia Woolf was in America at that time.

'In the 1970s the potter Judith Partridge had a studio in Mill House,' she remembers. 'Later the pottery was taken over by John Hawker, and in his time there were also a craft shop and an art gallery in Mill House.

'The actor Freddie Jones, who had relatives in the village, was a frequent visitor, and singer Joe Brown spent many an evening in the Abergavenny Arms when Connie and Albert Langridge had the pub.'

Ron Dartnell

In Rodmell flint is the predominate building material. Houses and barns, cow sheds, garages, garden and farmyard walls, sheds – even the quaint little privies still in some back gardens – are made from flints.

Ron Dartnell is the man the villagers call when a flint wall needs restoring or replacing.

Ron, born just up the road at Swanborough, in 1920, moved to Rodmell with his parents in 1941. After service with the RAF he returned to the village and in 1955 set up a general building business with Len Bennett, husband of shopkeeper Cissie. Len was one of the best flint workers in the business, 'a great craftsman', Ron says, and he taught his young colleague all he knew.

For more years than he cares to remember Ron has been the local flint wall specialist, in demand in flinty Downland villages up and down the valley. Even at his age he still, he says, has work enough for ten days a week.

Some Rodmell walls are around 300 years old, others were built by Ron within the last few years, using the techniques of the old master wall builders. He lays the flints by hand

Ron Dartnell with part of a new garden wall he built

was inexpensive, durable and attractive. The hard stone of nearly pure silica is found in roundish nodules which, when split, reveal all shades of marbled grey from pale dove to steely purple.

Ron usually uses knapped flints – split stones. 'You have to get the split in exactly the right place, or the flint will splinter to pieces,' he explains. But he has also restored walls where whole boulders are used, both randomly and in cobbled rows.

and eye and expertly mixes the pug with just the right amount of lime, or small ballast, to achieve a correct match, when restoring a wall.

Ron uses the same freehand method for new walls, having no time for the shuttering some builders now use to put up flint walling.

One of his regular clients says that it is always possible to identify a wall built by Ron, as his 'signature' runs right through it.

Ron has an arrangement with a local farmer to collect flints from his hilltop fields after ploughing.

Flint was always a popular building material in Downland communities. It

No two flint walls in Rodmell are exactly the same. Variations include brick string lines, chalk block or Caen stone inserts, haphazardly or straight laid stones, horizontally or vertically laid stones, flint and brick mixtures, different coloured mortars, pointed mortar and sculpted mortar.

Ron has seen many changes in the village and, a man who does not mince words, has no hesitation in deploring

A Rodmell wall of intact, prominently pointed flints

Square-knapped flint wall as on The Old Rectory

the actions of incoming townsfolk who move to the country and attempt to impose urban ways on rural communities.

'There are some,' Ron says darkly, 'who have come here and complained about the cows, the tractors and the farmyard smells! Now the last farm has gone from the village and there are new houses on the site.'

ACKNOWLEDGEMENTS

Special thanks are due to Pauline Cherry, Frank Dean and the late Jim Bartholomew, and to all those other residents who helped in the production of this village guide.

PICTURE CREDITS

Drawings on pages 2, 3, 4, 5, 14, 26, 27, 30 (top), 36, Pauline Cherry. Drawings on page 13, Lindel Organisation. Drawings on pages 19 and 21, Richard Kennedy. Drawing on page 6, Helen Fenton. Photographs on pages 41 and 42 loaned by Frank Dean. Photographs on page 45 loaned by Ron and Dorothy Medhurst. Photographs on pages 6, 18, 22, 32, 33, 34, 37, 38, 39, 40, 47, JEM. Postman Pat drawing on page 30, Celia Berridge.

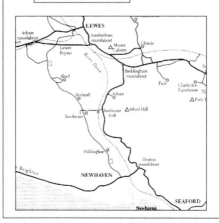

Rodmell notice board

● Gardens throughout the village are open to the public on the last Sunday in June each year. Teas are available, and there are plants for sale. ●

● RAMBLERS COMING DOWN-RIVER FROM LEWES ARE REMINDED THAT THERE IS NO RETURN BUS ON SUNDAY, AND THAT THE VILLAGE HAS NO STORE AND NO TEA SHOP. ●

● B&B? call 01273 474684 or 01273 477865